THE SCIENCE BEHIND
BATMAN'S
GROUND VEHICLES

by
Tammy Enz

BATMAN created by
Bob Kane with Bill Finger

SCIENCE BEHIND
BATMAN

CAPSTONE PRESS
a capstone imprint

Published by Capstone Press in 2016
A Capstone Imprint
1710 Roe Crest Drive
North Mankato, Minnesota 56003
www.mycapstone.com

STAR36689

Library of Congress Cataloging-in-Publication Data
Names: Enz, Tammy, author.
Title: The science behind Batman's ground vehicles / by Tammy Enz.
Description: North Mankato, Minnesota : Capstone Press, 2016. | 2016 | Series: DC
   super heroes. Science behind Batman | Audience: Ages 7-9. | Audience: K to grade 3.
   | Includes bibliographical references and index.
Identifiers: LCCN 2016002658| ISBN 9781515720348 (library binding) | ISBN
   9781515720409 (paperback) | ISBN 9781515720447 (ebook (pdf))
Subjects: LCSH: Motor vehicles—Design and construction—Juvenile literature. |
   Batman (Fictitious character)—Juvenile literature.
Classification: LCC TL147 .E595 2016 | DDC 629.2—dc23
LC record available at http://lccn.loc.gov/2016002658

Summary: Explores the real-world science and engineering connections to the features of Batman's road vehicles.

Editorial Credits
Christopher Harbo, editor; Hilary Wacholz, designer; Wanda Winch, media researcher;
Tori Abraham, production specialist

Artwork by Luciano Vecchio and Ethen Beavers

Photo Credits
Alamy: A.T. Willett, 12, ZUMA Press/Nancy Kaszerman, 15 (bottom); Courtesy of Boston Dynamics, 17; Defense Imagery Mgmt. Ops Center: Master Sgt. Jeremy Lock, 11; Newscom: Cal Sport Media/Paul Hebert, 16, Wenn.com/ZOB/CB2, 21, ZUMA Press/Sutton Motorsports, 9 (top), ZUMA PRESS/UPPA, 9 (b); Shutterstock: Jenoche, 7 (b); U.S. Air Force photo by Staff Sgt. Joseph Swafford Jr., 15 (t), U.S. Air Force photo by Staff Sgt. Bennie J. Davis III, 13 (left); U.S. Army photo by Spc. Kayla Benson, 19 (t); U.S. Secret Service, 19 (b); Wikimedia: BMK, 20, IFCAR, 7 (t)

Printed in China.
007727

TABLE OF CONTENTS

INTRODUCTION

SUPER HERO WHEELS

Batman drives eye-popping ground vehicles. They range from the sporty Batmobile to the speedy Batcycle. Both are packed with powerful engines, bulletproof tires, and other amazing features. Best of all, many of these features exist in the real world.

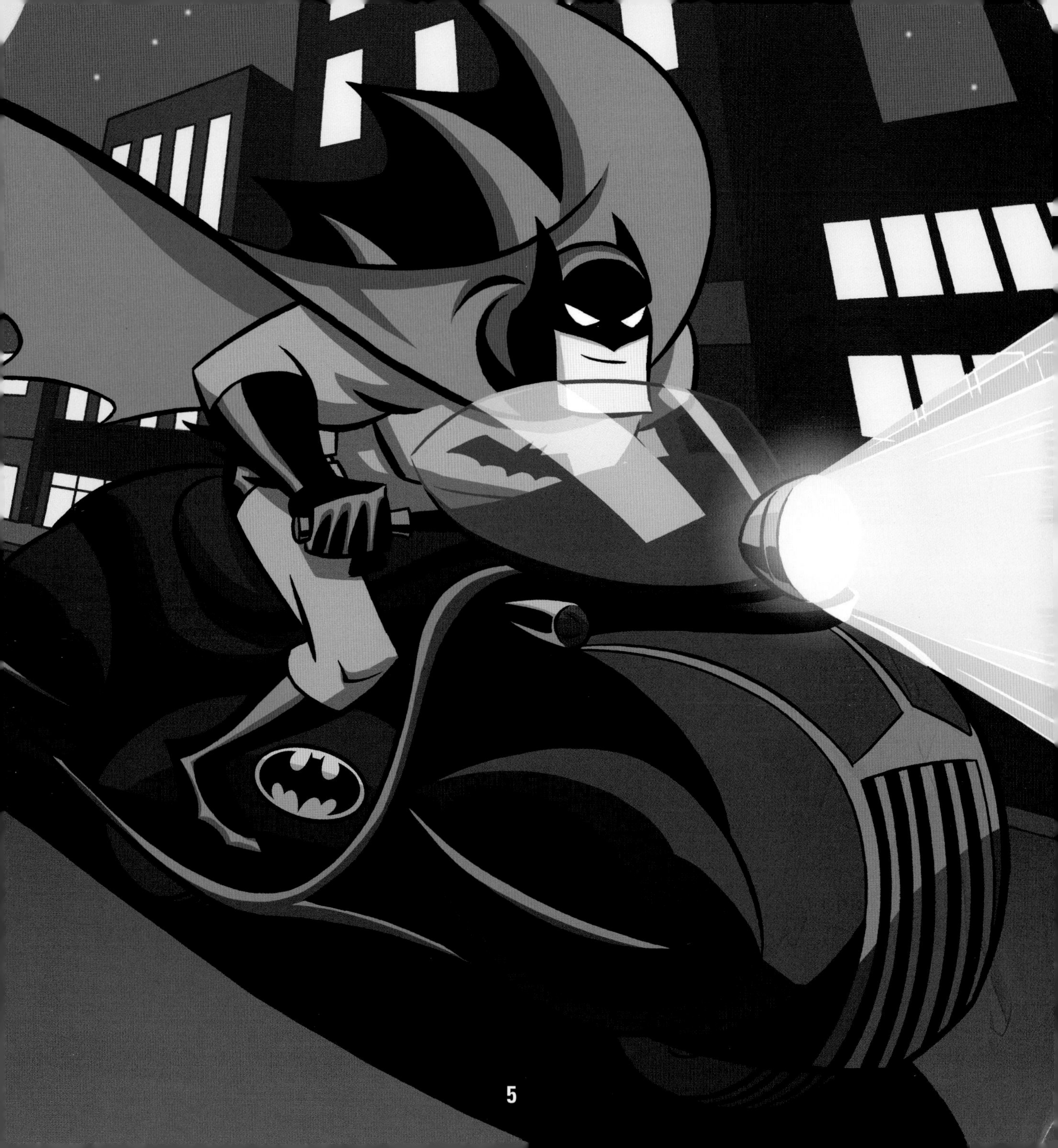

CHAPTER 1

POWER BOOSTS

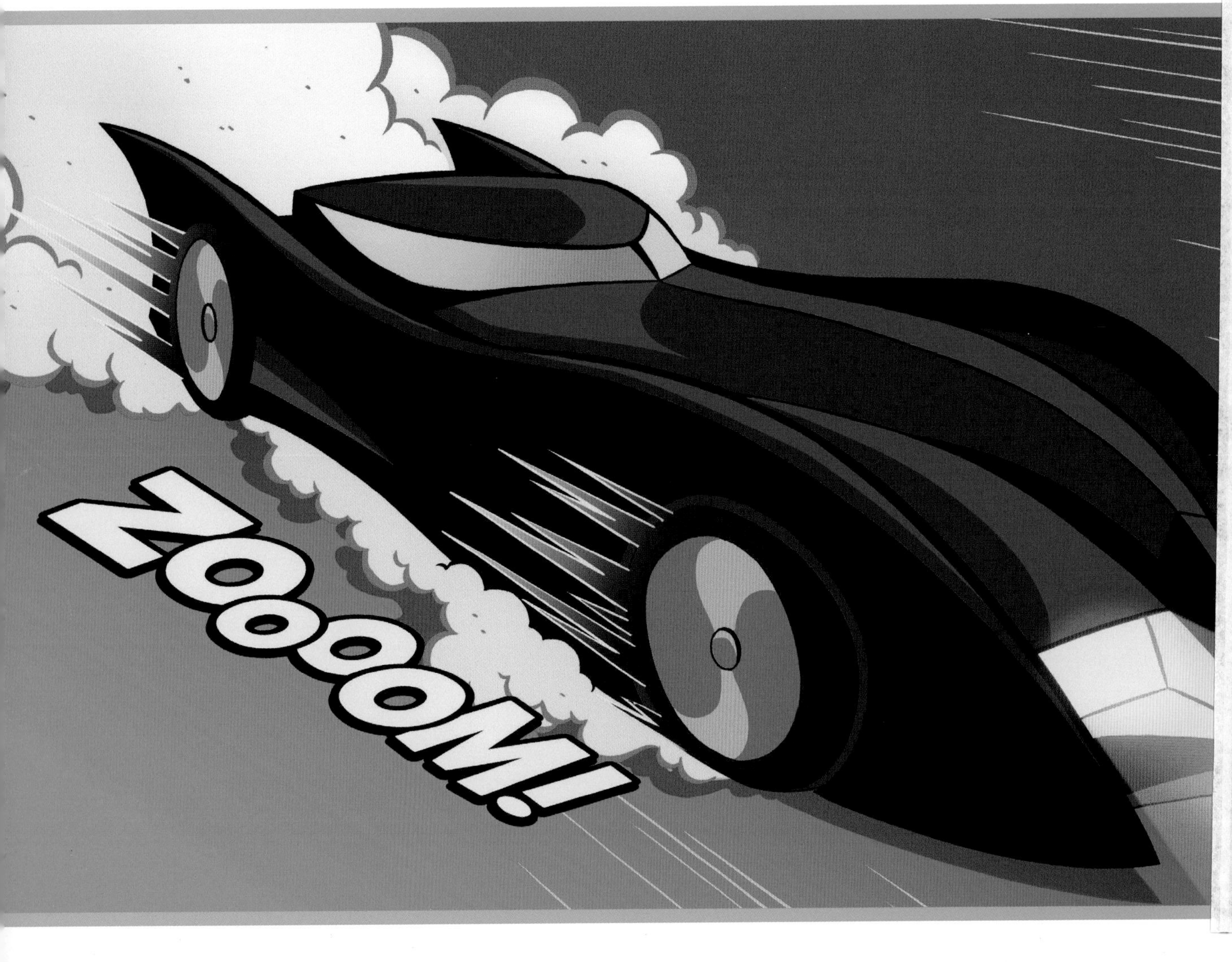
ZOOOOM!

Batman's vehicles often use **turbochargers** to chase down super-villains in Gotham City. Turbochargers boost engines in our world too. These devices pump extra air and gas into engines. They increase engine power by 30 to 40 percent.

The BMW 328i sedan is powered by a turbocharged engine.

FACT

Turbochargers have boosted car engines for more than 50 years. The 1962 Oldsmobile Jetfire was one of the first to use one.

turbocharger—a system that forces air through an engine to make a vehicle go faster

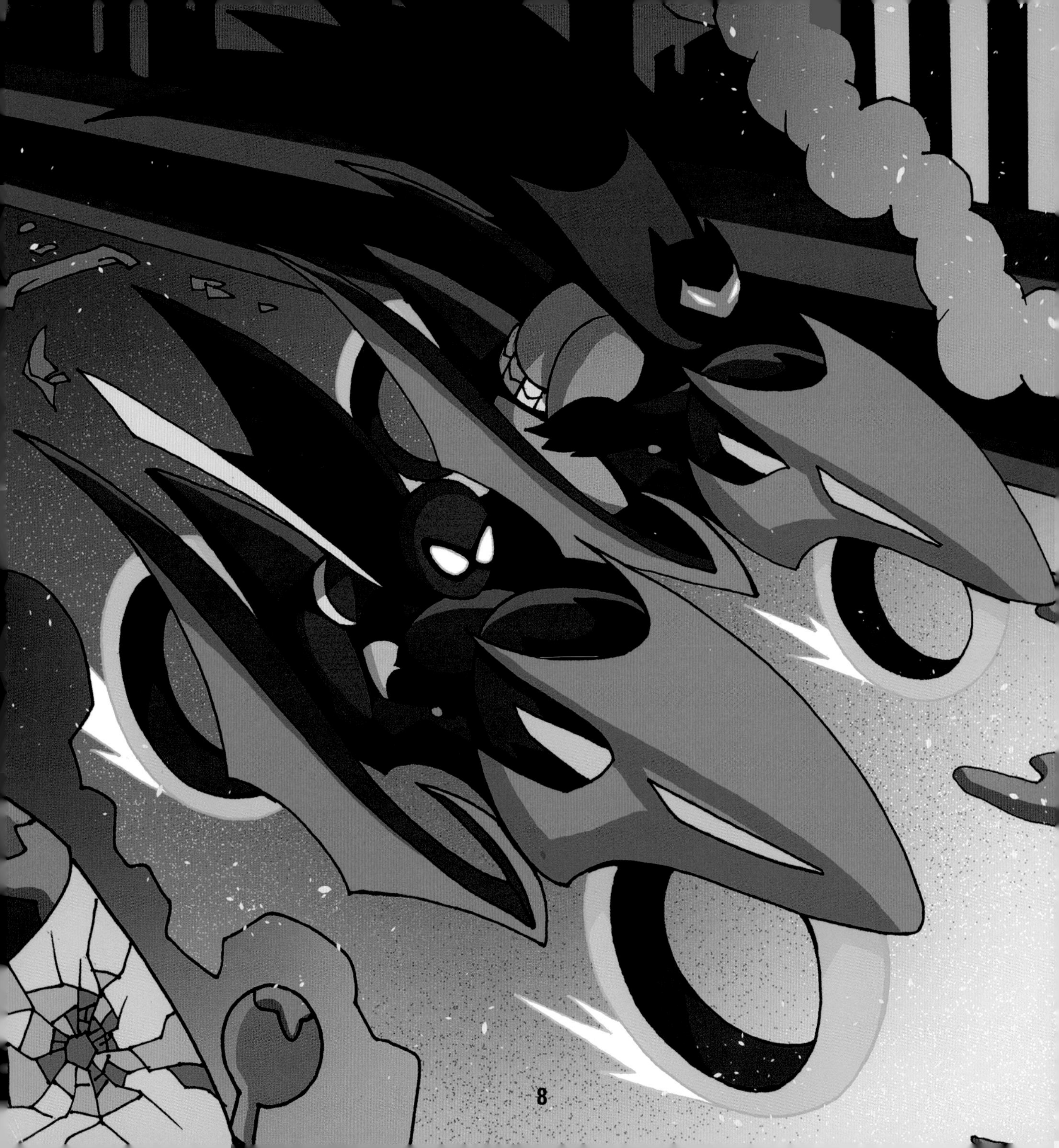

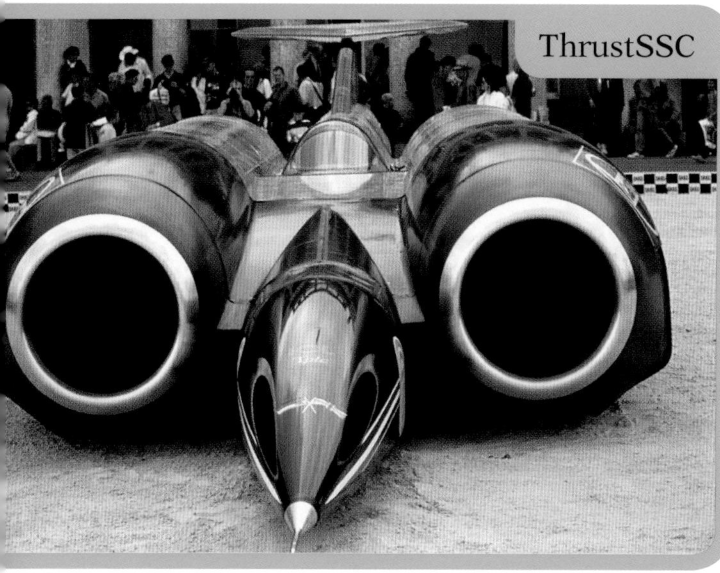

ThrustSSC

Rockets give Batman's vehicles amazing bursts of speed. In our world, some **experimental** cars use rockets too. The Thrust Supersonic Car (SSC) uses two huge jet engines. In 1997 it set a world record when it reached 763 miles (1,228 kilometers) per hour. It broke the speed of sound.

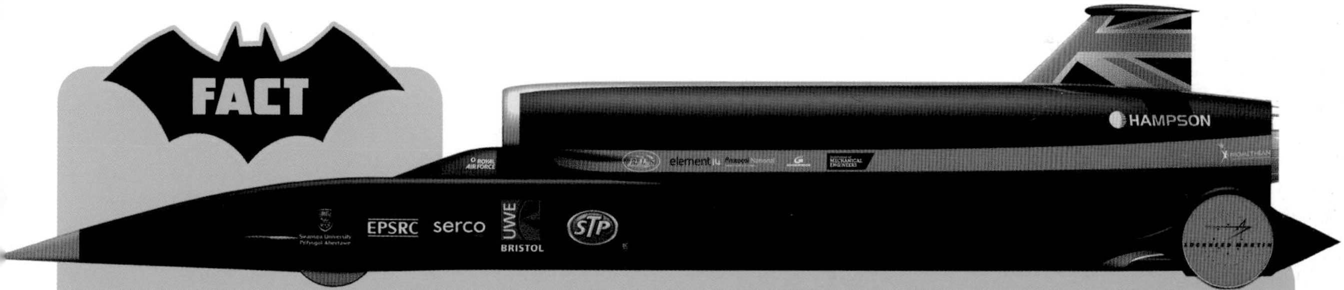
HAMPSON
EPSRC
serco
UWE
BRISTOL
STP

FACT

The Bloodhound SSC is being designed to go even faster than ThrustSSC. Its builders hope to reach more than 1,000 miles (1,609 km) per hour.

experimental—having to do with something that hasn't been tested fully

CHAPTER 2
HIDDEN CAPABILITIES

Batman's vehicles enter **stealth** mode by turning off lights and running quiet engines.

For the military, stealth aircraft can disappear from **radar**. A stealth aircraft's body is made with advanced materials and shapes. Its special design helps absorb and deflect radar signals.

The F-22 Raptor's body shape and covering help it stay hidden from radar.

stealth—having the ability to move secretly

radar—a device that uses radio waves to track the location of objects

The Batmobile's ejection seat keeps Batman safe in a crash. In fighter jets, a pilot pulls a handle to use an ejection seat. Explosive bolts blast off the cockpit **canopy**. A rocket then launches the pilot's seat high above the plane. Finally, a parachute carries the pilot safely to the ground.

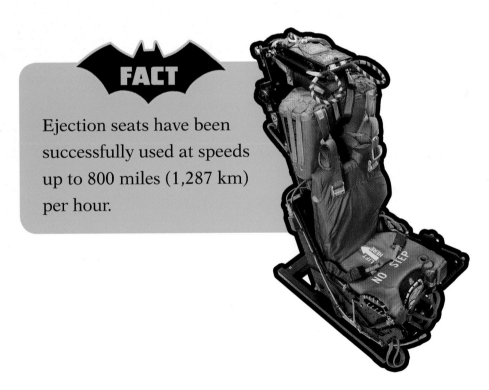

FACT

Ejection seats have been successfully used at speeds up to 800 miles (1,287 km) per hour.

canopy—the sliding cover over an airplane's cockpit

An Air Force pilot ejects from a fighter jet after guiding it safely away from an air show.

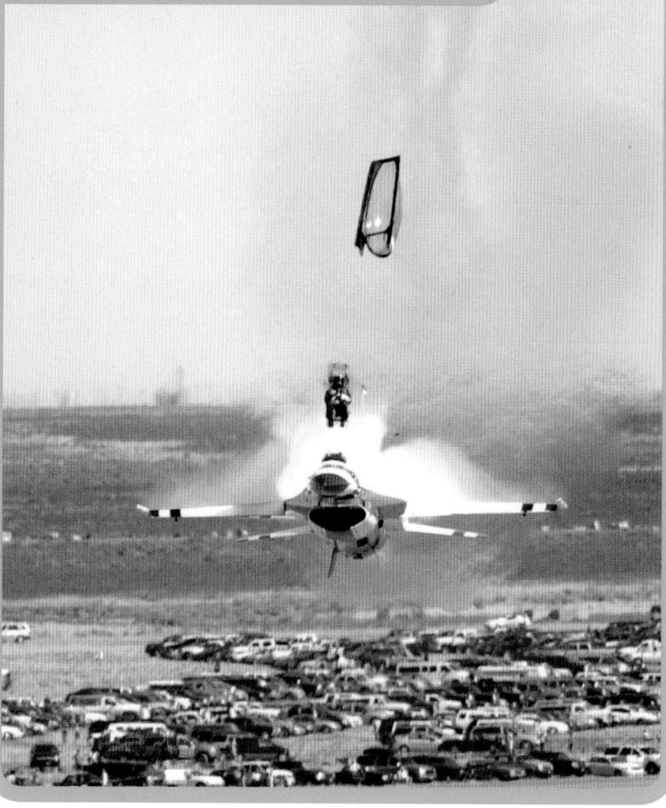

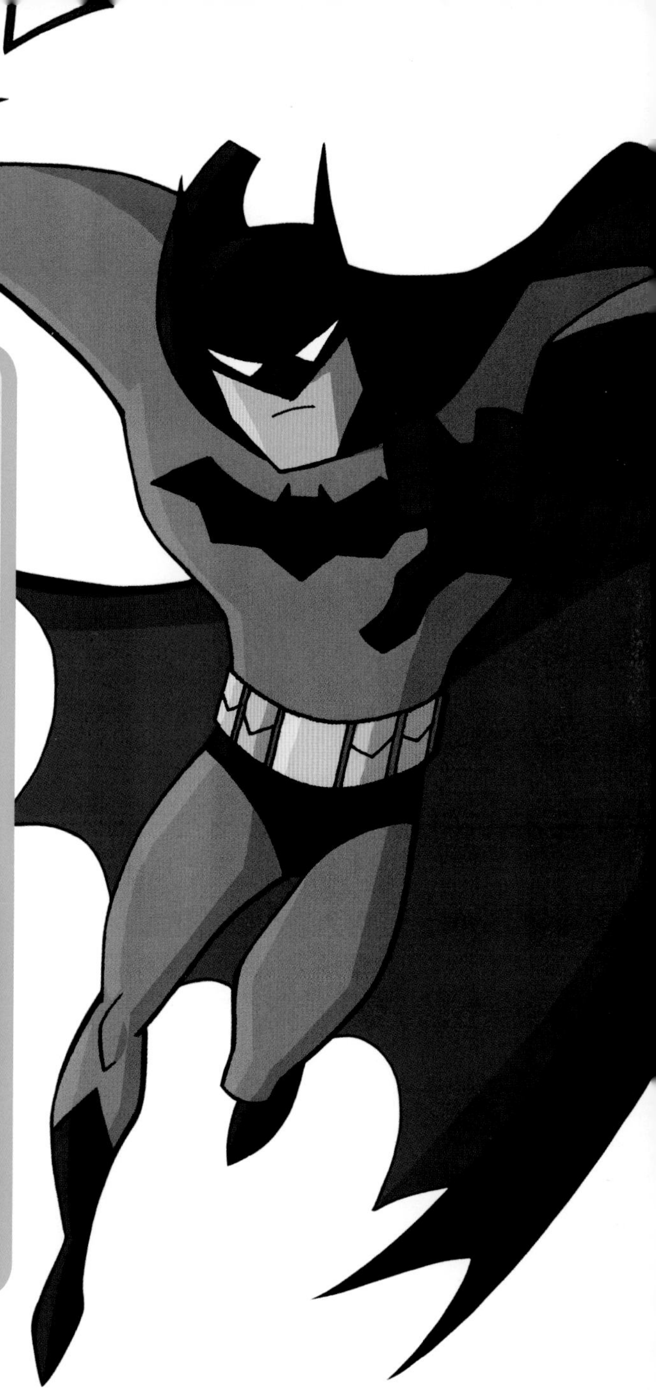

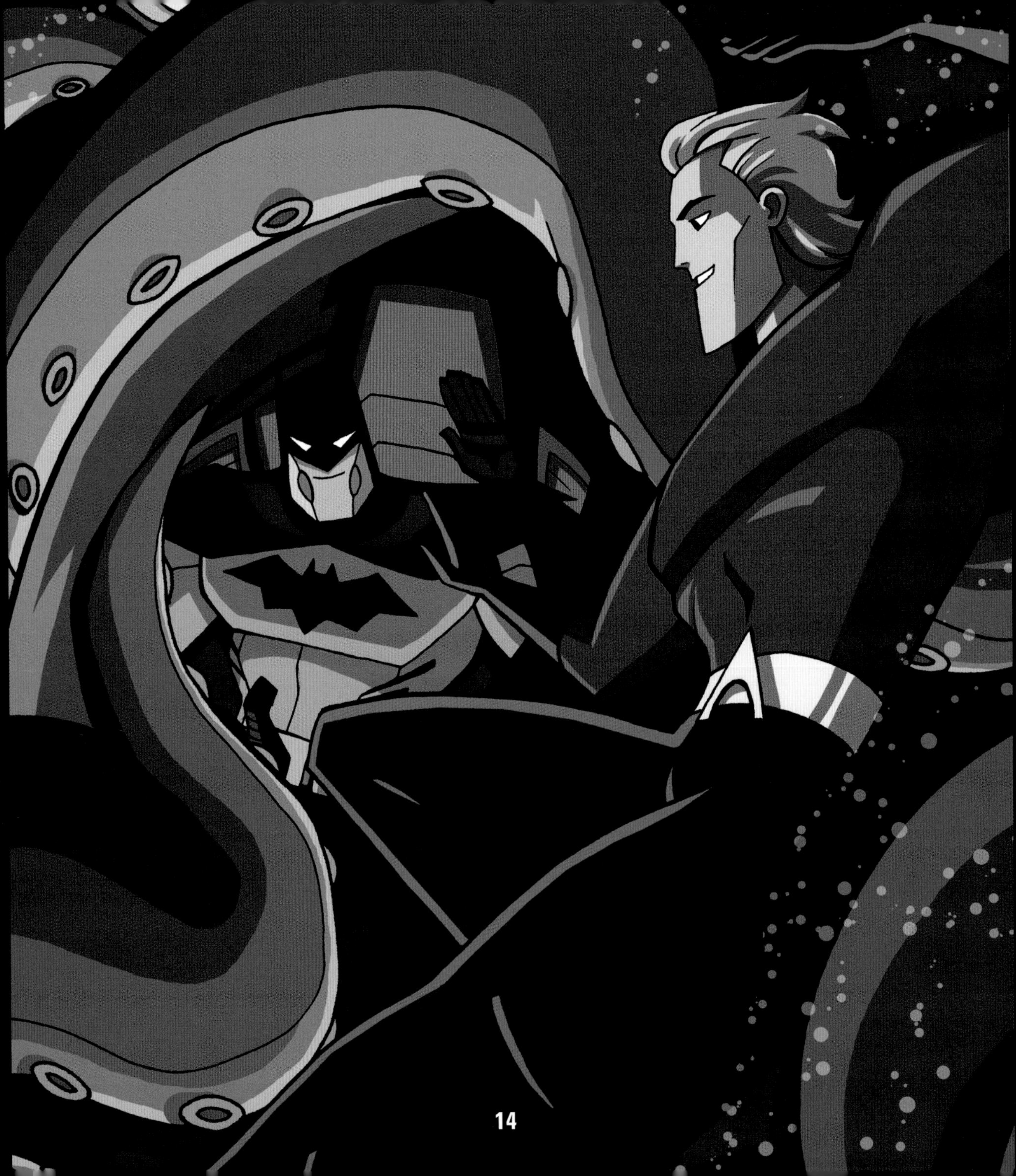

In the thick of action, Batman's ground vehicles sometimes change into boats or planes. Some modern vehicles do this too. The Gibbs Humdinga drives like a normal car on land. But in water its wheels fold up. Then jets push it through the water at more than 30 miles (48 km) per hour.

A Gibbs Humdinga glides across a marina.

FACT

The Terrafugia Transition is a flying car! It drives on land like a car, and it can unfold its wings and take flight.

When bridges crumble, the Batmobile never fails to leap the gap. Jumping real cars usually involves a ramp. A ramp helps a car gain enough upward force to counteract **gravity**. In 2009, Travis Pastrana used a ramp to jump 269 feet (82 meters). It was the world's longest jump with a car.

Travis Pastrana flies through the air during his record-breaking jump in 2009.

FACT

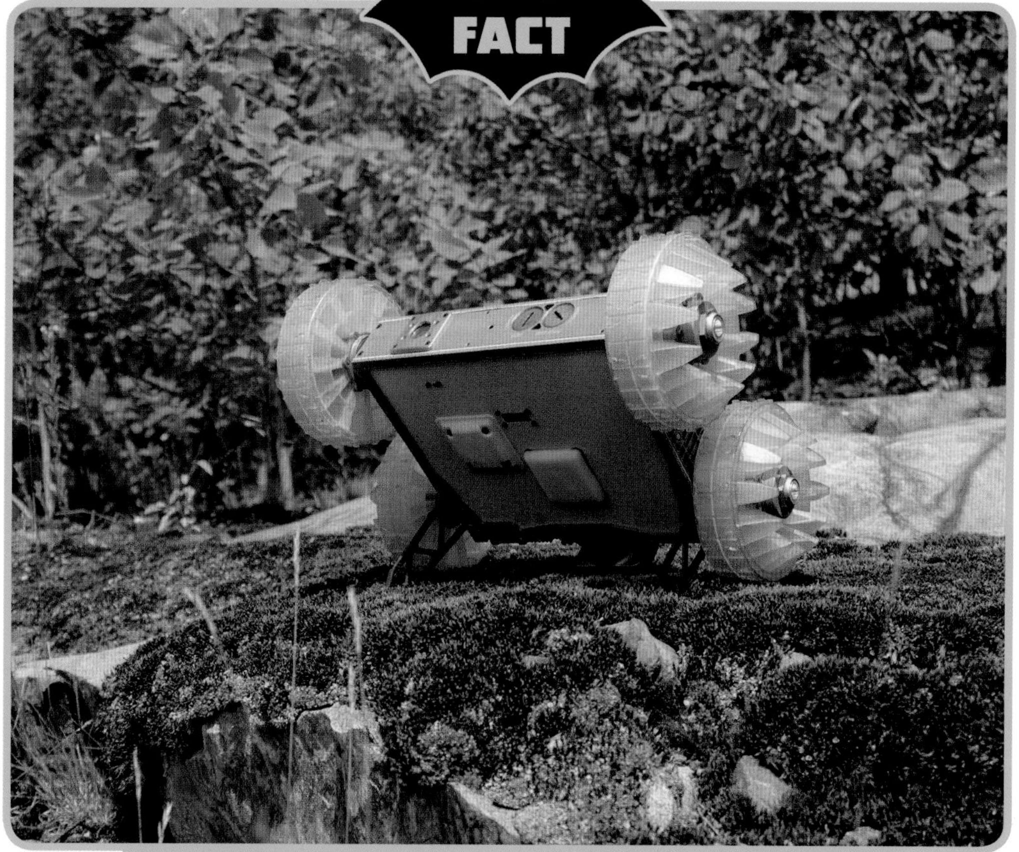

A **piston** on the back of the SandFlea allows it to jump without a ramp. The robotic car can leap 30 feet (9 m) straight up into the air.

gravity—a force that pulls objects with mass together

piston—a part inside a machine that moves up and down

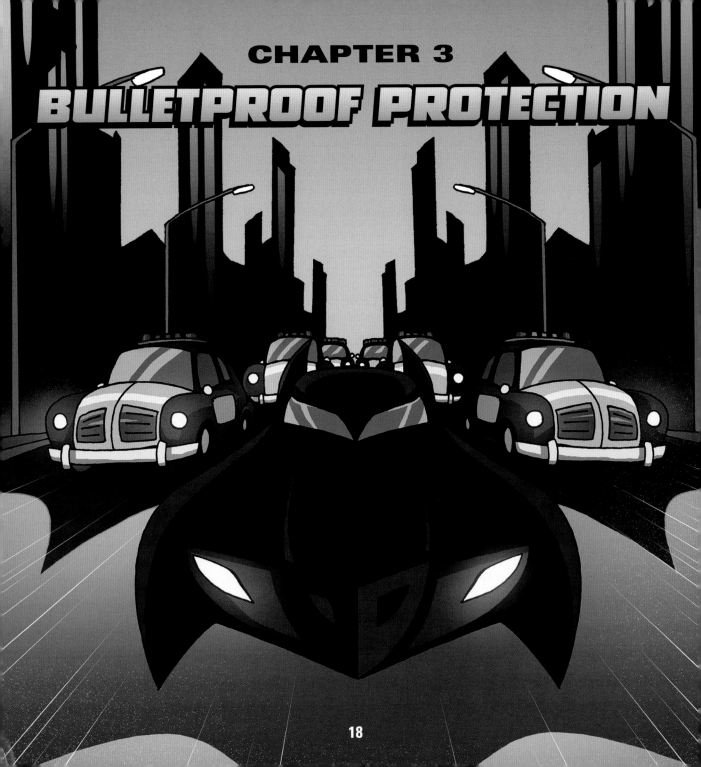

CHAPTER 3
BULLETPROOF PROTECTION

The Batmobile's body and windows deflect bullets. Many military vehicles have bulletproof windows too. These windows are made of a strong plastic sandwiched between regular glass. Bullets can break through the outer glass, but the plastic layer stops them.

A soldier peers through the bulletproof glass in an armored Humvee gun turret.

FACT

The U.S. president's limo is nicknamed "The Beast." It may be the only car in the world with armor as strong as the Batmobile's.

The tires on Batman's vehicles never go flat—even under gunfire. In the real world, **auxiliary** tires keep many cars rolling down the road. These tires have a solid inner ring. The ring carries the weight of the vehicle if the tire blows out.

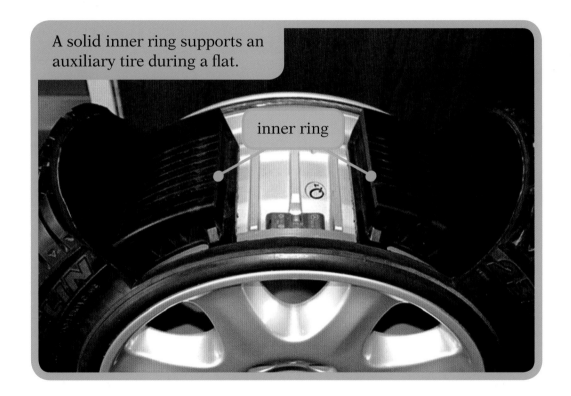

A solid inner ring supports an auxiliary tire during a flat.

inner ring

auxiliary—helping, or giving extra support

FACT

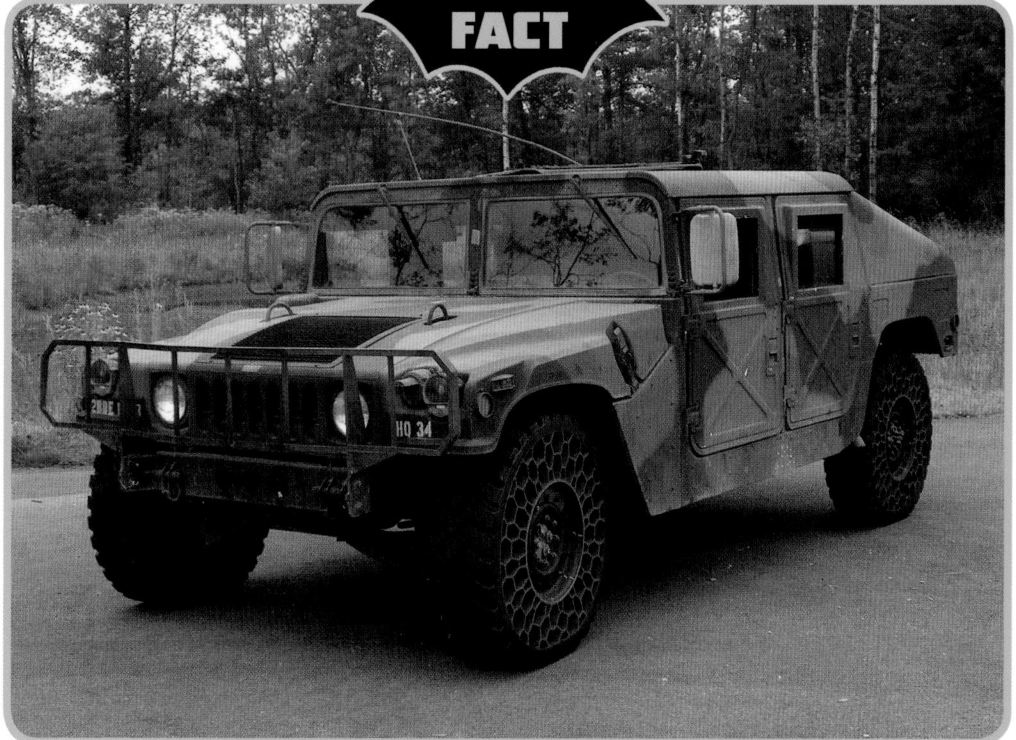
HQ 34

Engineers have designed an airless tire for the military. Its honeycombed pattern can withstand explosions.

Batman's vehicles rule the road with remarkable features. The real world science behind them is as amazing as the Dark Knight himself.

GLOSSARY

auxiliary (awg-ZIL-yur-ee)—helping, or giving extra support

canopy (KA-nuh-pee)—the sliding cover over an airplane's cockpit

experimental (ek-sper-uh-MEN-tuhl)—having to do with something that hasn't been tested fully

gravity (GRAV-uh-tee)—a force that pulls objects with mass together

piston (PIS-tuhn)—a part inside a machine that moves up and down

radar (RAY-dar)—a device that uses radio waves to track the location of objects

stealth (STELTH)—having the ability to move secretly

turbocharger (TUR-boh-char-juhr)—a system that forces air through an engine to make a vehicle go faster

READ MORE

Colson, Rob. *Tanks and Military Vehicles*. Ultimate Machines. New York: PowerKids Press, 2013.

Spilsbury, Richard. *Great Car Designs 1900-Today*. Iconic Designs. Chicago: Heinemann Raintree, 2016.

INTERNET SITES

FactHound offers a safe, fun way to find Internet sites related to this book. All of the sites on FactHound have been researched by our staff.

Here's all you you do:
Visit *www.facthound.com*
Type in this code: 9781515720348

INDEX

READ THEM ALL!

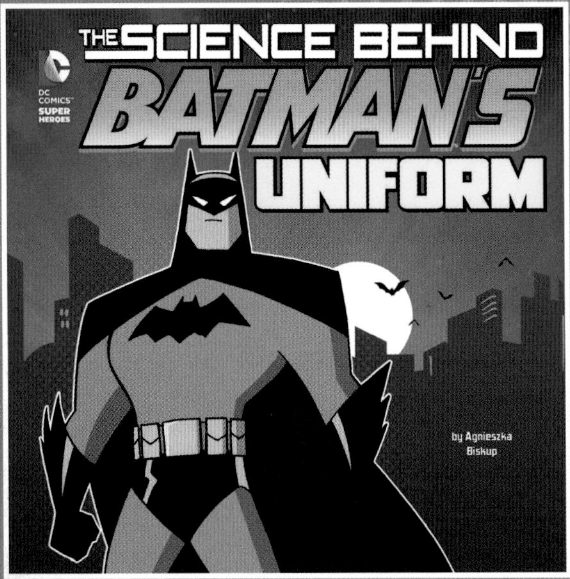

THE SCIENCE BEHIND
BATMAN'S
UNIFORM
DC COMICS SUPER HEROES
by Agnieszka Biskup

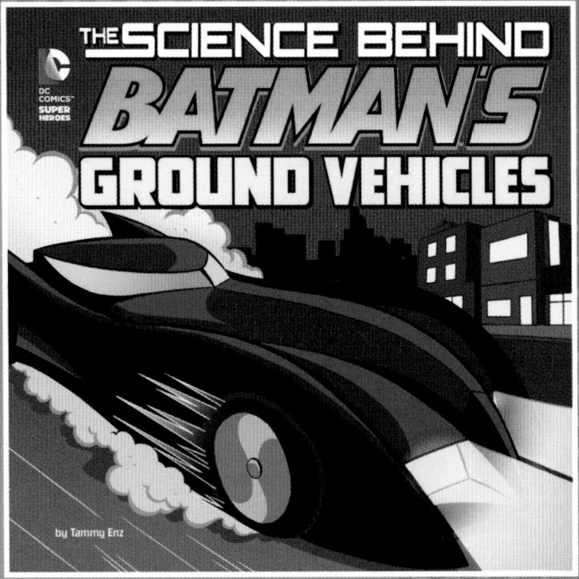

THE SCIENCE BEHIND
BATMAN'S
GROUND VEHICLES
DC COMICS SUPER HEROES
by Tammy Enz

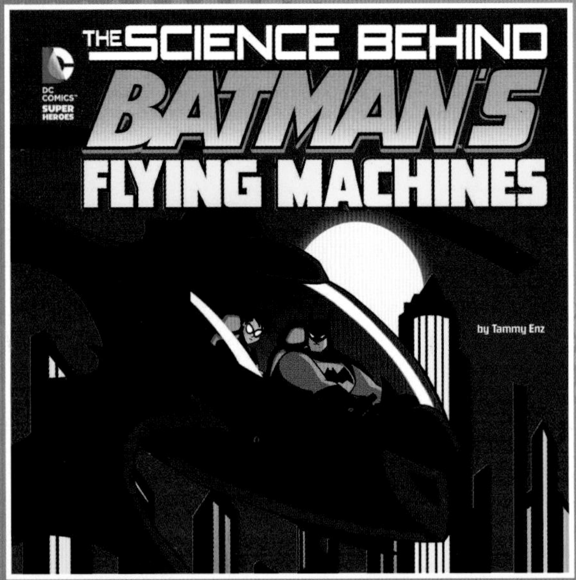

THE SCIENCE BEHIND
BATMAN'S
FLYING MACHINES
DC COMICS SUPER HEROES
by Tammy Enz

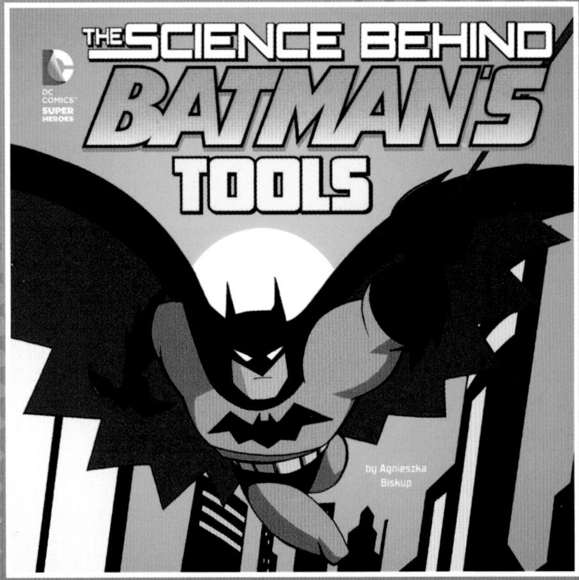

THE SCIENCE BEHIND
BATMAN'S
TOOLS
DC COMICS SUPER HEROES
by Agnieszka Biskup